IMAGES
of America

MILTON

The town landing in Milton as seen in 1897 from Godfrey's Wharf.

IMAGES
of America

MILTON

Paul Buchanan and Anthony Sammarco

ARCADIA

First published 1996
Copyright © Paul Buchanan and Anthony Sammarco, 1996

ISBN 0-7524-0286-2

Published by Arcadia Publishing,
an imprint of the Chalford Publishing Corporation
One Washington Center, Dover, New Hampshire 03820
Printed in Great Britain

Library of Congress Cataloging-in-Publication Data applied for

Contents

Acknowledgments

We would like to thank the officers and members of the Board of Directors of the Milton Historical Society for the use of the majority of the photographs in this book. The photograph collection of the Milton Historical Society is housed in the Milton Room at the Milton Public Library. Our sincere thanks go to: Nadine Leary, president; Paul Buchanan, vice-president; William Laughran, vice-president; Kevin Donahue, treasurer; Carolyn Thornton, secretary; and Directors Edith Clifford, Brian Doherty, Robert and Kathy Hale, Richard Heath, Jeannette Peverly, Margaret Recanzone, and Anne Thompson.

Our thanks for the interest shown in this book and their continued support also go to: Daniel Ahlin; Helen Buchanan; Glenn Coffman, director of Milton Public Library; William Dillon; the Reverend Thomas C. Foley (pastor, Saint Mary's Church); Nancy Foss Heath; Joseph Kennedy, M.D.; the late Mary Lee Evans Kimball; Eunice Laughran; William Leary; Judith McGillicuddy; Wesley and Sunny Merritt; the late Russell Peverly; Dana Ricciardi of the Forbes House Museum; Anthony and Mary Mitchell Sammarco; Rosemary Sammarco; Sylvia Sandeen; George Thompson; and William Varrell.

Introduction

European travelers, explorers, and settlers were in the area now known as Milton since early in the seventeenth century, and the written records of Thomas Merton and others suggest visits as early as the fall of 1621. The settling of Dorchester in 1630 includes the section south of the Neponset River known as Unquity-Quisset by the Neponset tribe of the Massachusetts Indians. By 1662, almost a generation after the first settlers arrived on what was to be known as Milton Hill, the General Court established the area as a separate town to be known as Milton.

Reverend Peter Thacher was ordained as the first minister in 1678 in what was now a well-settled country town where the principal endeavor of the inhabitants was farming. Additionally, fishing and some activity at the several mills which developed along the Neponset provided further economic growth. These mills, dating as early as 1634, included fulling mills, gun powder mills, and grist and saw mills. Indeed, Milton's grist mill was the first in the country.

By the eighteenth century, Milton was a reasonably prosperous agricultural community. Milton Village came into existence as the century developed with paper mills now joining the "husbandry" mills. A small shipbuilding industry was established near Gulliver's Creek. Commercial activities came to the Village when Daniel Vose opened his general store. As the century advanced, the area grew and a manufacturing industry developed, producing the first pianoforte, bass viol, and artificial leg. It was during this period that summer residents first began to come to the area. Several successful merchants and two Royal Governors of the Massachusetts Bay Colony from the Town of Boston chose to reside in Milton during the heat of the summer months.

As the colonies moved towards independence, the British Crown imposed ever-increasing restrictions, with the Bay Colony being forbidden to hold town meetings. Finally, delegates from several towns in Suffolk County held a gathering at Vose's Tavern in Milton Village and adopted a document known as the Suffolk Resolves which, after being brought to the Continental Congress by Paul Revere, became the basis for the Declaration of Independence.

By the end of the Revolutionary period, Milton had developed a prosperity based on agriculture, but with substantial industrial development at the Upper Falls in Mattapan and the Lower Falls in the Village. There was also vigorous commercial and shipping activity.

The nineteenth century brought many changes to Milton. The power of the Neponset River was tapped to allow industrial growth. The farms were now producing for the rapidly expanding urban market in Boston. Milton's first post office was opened in 1803. To build the Bunker Hill

Monument and then satisfy the burgeoning demand for granite to be used in new buildings in Boston, the granite quarries were tapped. The Granite Railway, America's first railway, was built, as was Railway Village, later to be called East Milton.

The development of Milton between 1860 and 1940 was tremendous. Milton grew from a small but prosperous farming community to a well-built and affluent suburb of Boston, with the aid of the Old Colony Railroad and the Massachusetts Bay Transportation Authority's "Red Line." The farms gave way to not only summer estates on Milton Hill, Canton Avenue, and Brush Hill Road, but also to smaller developments that attracted a population as diverse in its ethnic background as in its economic status.

Milton is outlined here in the eighty years following the Civil War as a town rich in natural resources such as the Neponset River, Houghton's Pond, and the Blue Hills and other open land protected by public agencies. The area is enriched by its wide array of architectural styles, from the grandest mansion to the most humble of bungalow-style houses. But the town's most important asset is, and has always been, its people.

One

Milton Village

Photographed at the turn of the century, the Neponset River divided Dorchester (on the right) and Milton. The boathouse of John Collins and the former Preston Chocolate Mill can be seen on the right. In the distance, one can see the Hotel Milton, an inn located at the bridge crossing the Neponset River; it was here that the first local Catholic mass was said in 1840.

The Suffolk Resolves House was on Adams Street, to the right of the present Associates Building in Milton Village. Built by Daniel Vose, a merchant, there was a grocery store and an inn on the first floor, with his residence above. On September 9, 1774, the Suffolk Resolves were drafted here, and were later delivered by Paul Revere to the Continental Congress in Philadelphia. In 1950, the house was moved to Canton Avenue and is now the headquarters of the Milton Historical Society.

The Crehore House was built by Benjamin Crehore (1765–1832) on Adams Street in Milton Village. Crehore, a mechanical genius, manufactured the first pianoforte, bass viol, and artificial leg in the United States in this house. His fame and success were ensured, but he repossessed the artificial leg from Dean Weymouth, a veteran of the War of 1812, for non-payment!

The Baker Chocolate Mill, seen from Eliot Street, was established in 1765 on the Dorchester side of the Neponset River. Known as the "Old Stone Mill," the granite structure was built in 1813 and the company housed there was a major employer of local residents. Gannett's grist mill, on the Milton side of the Neponset River, can be seen here on the right.

Two women pass Durrell's General Store in this view looking up Adams Street from Milton Village in 1865. The rise of Milton Hill is far steeper than today.

The paper mill, on the left, was built in the mid-eighteenth century for Jeremiah Smith, a manufacturer of paper. On the right is the former home of Dr. Jonathan Ware, owner of the Ware Chocolate Mill. It later was the home of H. Clifford Gallagher, a president of the Baker Chocolate Company. This is the present site of the Humbolt Moving and Storage Company.

High Street, originally known as "The Back Lane," connects Eliot Street and Canton Avenue. These late eighteenth-century houses added greatly to the charm of Milton Village.

John Swift's Hat Shop, on the right, was where beaver top hats were made in the early nineteenth century. Beside it is the old Babcock Tavern.

The first location of the Milton Public Library was in this house at the corner of Adams and Wharf Streets. It was not until the Associates Building, designed by Rotch & Tilden, was completed in 1881 that the library moved into more spacious accommodations.

The Neponset River, seen from Forbes' Wharf in 1886, had a bucolic quality as it passed Milton Village. Named for the Neponset tribe of the Massachusetts Indians, the river was an important source of water power as early as 1634, when a dam was erected for Stoughton's grist mill, the first in this country.

The first town landing on the Neponset River was at Gulliver's Creek. The reed marshes that banked the river still grow in abundance and a boat ride down the river still has a soothing and relaxing quality.

A spur of the Old Colony Railroad ran from Dorchester to Mattapan. The railroad tracks paralleled Eliot Street and provided passenger service to Milton by the time of the Civil War. This stretch of track is between the Milton and Central Avenue stations.

The train that served Milton puffed clouds of smoke as it approached Milton Village from Cedar Grove in Dorchester. Train service between Milton and Boston was a major factor in the suburban development of the town between 1885 and 1920.

Looking toward Adams Street at Milton Village, the Webb Mill can be seen in the distance. At one time there were four manufacturers of chocolate at the Lower Mills: Baker's Chocolate (established 1765), Preston's Chocolate (1768), Ware's Chocolate (1840), and Webb Chocolate, formerly Webb & Twombley Chocolate (1843). By 1881, all of these competitors were absorbed into the Walter Baker Chocolate Company.

Henry Lillie Pierce (1825–1896) was president of the Walter Baker Chocolate Company from 1854 until his death in 1896. An astute businessman, he increased the chocolate manufactory forty fold by the time of his death and created a complex of mill buildings producing chocolate and cocoa. The Lower Mills were renamed "Pierce Square" in his honor in 1896.

Looking east from Hutchinson Field on Adams Street to Milton Hill, the view toward the harbor is as panoramic and breathtaking today as it was a century ago. Blanketed with a fresh covering of snow, the hill rolls toward the marshes before reaching the harbor.

A painter records, in oils, the beauty of the Neponset River a century ago.

The Milton Hill House was on Eliot Street, overlooking the Neponset River. The original inn was a columned Greek Revival building that was but three minutes from the train station. It was said in an advertisement that by "a careful selection of guests . . . the management has during the past ten years supplied the comforts and attractions of a home of refinement."

The front parlor of the Milton Hill House had all the comforts of home! A gasolier and table lamp lit the dark, and rocking chairs and wicker chairs placed in the public rooms encouraged interaction among the residents. The Milton Hill House catered to "Persons who wish to live outside of the city in the spring before opening their country houses for the summer, or in the autumn before moving into town for the winter."

A woman, with her skirts billowing in the wind, bicycles past the Milton Hill House on Eliot Street.

Dudley Talbot (left) and John Talbot sit in a horse-drawn wagon that was used to deliver the groceries purchased from their store, Talbot's, at Milton Village. In the background Cedar Grove in Dorchester can be seen.

The delivery wagon of the Milton Fruit Store is parked in front of the store on Adams Street. Operated by Mr. Simonetti, fine quality fruit was available from this greengrocer, but only in season.

The Milton Fruit Store was located in the Martin Building, owned by Henry B. Martin. A large green-and-white-striped awning could be unfurled to shade the fruit from the summer sun.

Everett's Market was another shop in Milton Village. Photographed in 1927, the market was in the Collins Building, which was next to the Johnson Building. An automobile heads up Adams Street toward the junction of Adams Street and Randolph and Canton Avenues.

Looking toward the entrance to the Milton station on the surface trolley line, the Suffolk Resolves House can be seen on the right, shaded by two huge trees. On the left is the electrician's shop of F.J. King & Son.

Looking from Adams Street into the Lower Mills, the snow-covered tree branches of this winter scene seem to guard the Associates Building. The building, designed by Rotch & Tilden and built in 1882, featured tall arched windows. On the left is the Administration Building of the Baker Chocolate Company. It was designed by George Shepard and built in 1919.

Ice fishing, whereby one cuts a hole in the ice covering a river or pond, has gone on for centuries on the Neponset River.

The Milton station was a long brick-and-granite building that offered shelter for those taking the train to Boston. After the line became the surface trolley line connecting the Ashmont station and Mattapan, the Milton station was demolished.

The Neponset River overflowed its banks in 1955, causing flooding in Milton Village. Here, parking meters for cars are covered by over 2 feet of water!

The Neponset River passes under the bridge that connects Dorchester and Milton. On the right is the Pierce Mill of Baker's Chocolate, now remodeled as apartments. On the left is Pierce Square, the junction of Dorchester Avenue and Washington and Adams Streets, which was named in honor of Henry L. Pierce in 1896.

Looking from the bridge on Adams Street, the platform of the Milton station is marked by billboards that project from the flood waters.

Two
Milton Hill

The view toward the Neponset River from the summer house of J. Malcolm Forbes on Adams Street is spectacular.

"Unquity" was the summer house of Royal Governor Thomas Hutchinson (1711–1780). A hip-roofed one-story house with a pedimented colonnade, the estate, later owned by the Russell family, was extensively remodeled in the late nineteenth century.

The Belcher House was the summer house of Royal Governor Jonathan Belcher (1681–1757). It was located on Adams Street, near Belcher Circle.

The Gooch-Churchill House is an impressive Colonial house on Adams Street near Churchill's Lane. Built in 1740, the house was separated from Adams Street by a rough stone wall.

The Nathan Babcock House was built in 1753 on Adams Street, near Father Carney Road. A small gambrel-roofed cottage, it has not changed in the eight decades since it was photographed.

The Rising Sun Tavern was located at the corner of Adams Street and Canton Avenue. Built by Samuel Vose as a tavern, it was a popular stopping place for stages traveling south on Adams Street. By the turn of the century, the tavern was remodeled for Litman & Brother Tailors, and had rooms for rent above. The site is today the Chapman, Cole and Gleason Funeral Home.

The Cabot-Robbins-Morton House was built on what is now Morton Road in the late eighteenth century. It was home to Edward Hutchinson Robbins, a lawyer and founder of Milton Academy. In this c. 1870 photograph, the gardens had a lattice-work summerhouse flanked by stone urns.

Dr. Amos Holbrook (1754–1842) was an early doctor who inoculated town residents against smallpox. Built in 1800 on Adams Street, his house was later the home of Mary Forbes Cunningham, who left the Cunningham Fund to benefit the residents of Milton.

The foyer of the Holbrook House, while owned by Mary Forbes Cunningham, contained porcelain garden seats exported from China, palms, oriental rugs, and a Chinese lantern. The mirror on the right was once owned by Governor Hutchinson and was donated to the Milton Historical Society by Mary Rivers. It now hangs in the Milton Public Library.

Robert Bennet Forbes (1804–1889) built this summer house for his mother, Mary Perkins Forbes, in 1833 on Adams Street. Designed by Isaiah Rogers, the house was greatly enlarged when a third story was added in 1872–73 by Peabody & Stearns. Today, the Robert Bennet Forbes House is open to the public as an example of one family's life in Milton over the course of a century.

Miss Mary Bowditch Forbes was the daughter of Alice Bowditch and J. Murray Forbes. A noted collector of Lincoln memorabilia, she had a great affinity for her dogs, many of whom sat at the table during dinner.

Congressman Rathbone addresses a crowd from a tree stump on the Forbes Estate in 1926. Rathbone's parents, Clara Harris and Major Henry R. Rathbone, were in the box with Abraham and Mary Todd Lincoln at Ford's Theatre in Washington, D.C., when Lincoln was assassinated. After the Lincoln Log Cabin was built, Miss Mary Forbes hosted the public annually on February 12 for tours of the cabin.

The Lincoln Log Cabin was built by Thomas Murdock of Milton to house Miss Mary Forbes' growing collection of Lincoln memorabilia. With paintings, prints, etchings, and Lincoln-related artifacts, this reproduction of Lincoln's birthplace drew visitors from near and far.

The Glover-Gardner House is at 144 Adams Street, opposite Randolph and Canton Avenues. Built by Dr. Samuel Glover in 1800, the house has superb views toward the harbor.

The Benjamin Dudley House was a Greek Revival house on Adams Street with impressive Doric columns supporting twin-pedimented gables.

The John Henry Brooks House, known as "Wayside Farm," was an impressive Italianate mansion on Adams Street. A circular carriage drive, a fountain, and flower-holding urns made for a comfortable Milton estate in the late nineteenth century.

Local lore has it that this is the Hutchinson House on Adams Street after being "somewhat remodeled." The house is a panoply of gables, stick-style detailing, and piazzas that wrap around the house. During World War II, the house was the headquarters of the Milton Red Cross.

The Swift House is a late eighteenth-century house on Adams Street that was remodeled by architect John A. Fox of Dorchester. After adding a two-story bay, a new entrance porch, and a rear carriage house, the estate remains as charming as it was before remodeling.

Miss Mary Rogers Swift poses beside her Christmas tree in 1896. The daughter of John Swift, a hat maker, she lived in great comfort. Together with her sister Elizabeth, she left a bequest to the town known as the "Swift Charity." She also bequeathed the "old fashioned bookcase in the back parlor, thought to have been owned by the last Colonial Governor" to the Milton Public Library. This secretary desk is now in the Trustees Room at the library.

"Brookmount" was the estate of the Safford family. Built on Westside Road, the house was set in the midst of extensive grounds.

The gardens of "Brookmount" included formal parterres with a reflecting pool and large stone urns. Photographed in 1910, Dutch bulbs proclaim the arrival of spring.

At the corner of Adams and Hutchinson Streets is the birthplace of former United States President George Walker Bush. This large, shingle-style house was rented by the Prescott Bushes for one year, and the future president was born there in 1924.

Looking past this classical gate are Hutchinson Field and the Neponset River. Now protected by the Trustees of Reservations, the land was donated by Mary Forbes Cunningham and her brothers to remain forever open land for the benefit of the public.

Three
East Milton

The Blue Bell Tavern was built in "Railway Village," as East Milton was originally known. Built on the present site of the East Milton Post Office, it must have been a popular place on pay day for the stone workers in the quarries at West Quincy! The Granite Railway, America's first railroad, was initiated by Gridley Bryant, who invented the movable truck used on the eight-wheel rail car.

The East Milton train station was at the intersection of Granite Avenue and Adams Street. A train approaches East Milton as a young boy awaits the arrival of the passengers from Boston.

Passengers wait at the East Milton stop to board the last train in East Milton. Discontinued in 1940, train service was severely affected by the automobile.

A train derailment in 1900 was photographed at East Milton while gawkers came by foot and by bicycle to see the destruction firsthand.

The granite that was quarried in West Quincy was often stored in a yard on Granite Avenue in East Milton. In the distance can be seen the belfry of the East Milton Congregational Church.

The Blue Bell Tavern was built of the granite quarried in West Quincy. A commodious building, it offered not only a warming drink and a hearty meal, but also rooms to let above. Granite was used even to construct markers for walks and drives.

The Felt Blacksmith Shop was built at the corner of Adams and Squantum Streets. Here the blacksmith employed by the granite concern would forge the necessary iron. In the twentieth century, this building was converted to a duplex house. Note the mother with her baby carriage to the left.

Granite Avenue, on the left, intersected Adams Street at East Milton. The railroad crossing is marked and the Blue Bell Tavern can be seen on the right.

Adams Street, looking towards East Milton Square, was an unpaved street that had railroad tracks so the granite could be moved easily by rail.

The Glover-Gardner House on Adams Street is the oldest house in East Milton.

A group of East Milton women posed in 1864 for this photograph. From left to right are: Mrs. John Emerson, Miss Emma Emerson, Mrs. Hilary Bygrave, Miss Clara Babcock, Miss Susan Brokenshire, Mrs. Charles R. Young, Mrs. Albert A. Brackett, Miss M. Alice Babcock, and Mrs. Frederick M. Hamlin.

East Milton Square in 1870 was fairly rural with stone walls, tree-lined streets, and no evidence of the expressway!

This photograph shows Adams Street looking towards East Milton Square, with Foster Lane on the left and Granite Place on the right.

East Milton Square in 1900 was a far less busy intersection than it is now. Adams Street was a tree-lined way with the firehouse on the right.

East Milton Square is shown here c. 1940, looking down Granite Avenue toward Adams Street. The cars parked on the left, and the street would eventually give way to the Southeast Expressway.

Looking north from East Milton Square, Granite Avenue is being excavated for the new expressway. The East Milton Post Office, built in 1937 on the site of the Blue Bell Tavern, can be seen on the left.

By 1954, the deep excavations for the expressway led to a cavernous valley that divided Milton along Granite Avenue.

East Milton Square before the Southeast Expressway was more compact than today. Adams Street and Granite Avenue intersect with ample parking for train commuters and shoppers.

In 1956, after the completion of the Southeast Expressway, East Milton Square was divided by rail embankments that protected pedestrians and automobiles from the depressed expressway.

Four
Around Milton Centre

This World War I memorial was sculpted by Daniel Chester French and placed on a granite plinth on the town common to the left of the First Congregational Church. The inscription, carved in stone, reads: "Take up our quarrel with the foe; To you with failing hands we throw The torch; be yours to hold it high."

The Milton Town Hall was an elaborate Victorian building with a massive Romanesque arch for an entrance and a soaring belfry on the left. The building, designed by Hartwell & Tilden and built in 1878, was on Canton Avenue, between the First Parish Church, Unitarian and the First Congregational Church. The town hall was demolished in 1968, and a gazebo erected by Baron Hugo in memory of his wife, Edith Esabella Hamilton Lira, marks its site.

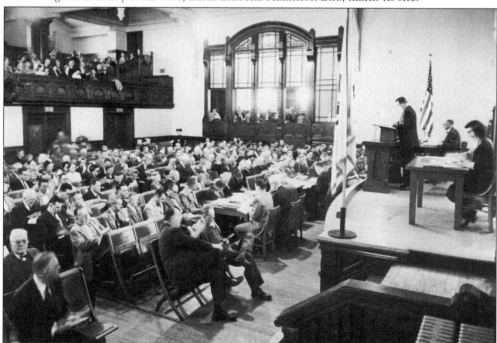

In 1636, selectmen were elected at the first town meeting in Dorchester, Massachusetts. Milton's town meetings are seen as a perpetuation of the original. This photograph shows a town meeting in 1955.

The 250th Anniversary Committee of Milton met in October 1912 outside the town hall for this photograph. From the left to right are: John Alden Lee, Dr. Freeland D. Lillie, Nathaniel T. Kidder, Arthur H. Tucker, and Andrew H. Ward.

Milton Town Hall was the site of many town celebrations, dances, and even horticultural exhibits. Local farmers and horticulturalists displayed fruits and vegetables on long tables in 1912.

The Milton Public Library is an impressive building at the corner of Canton Avenue and Reedsdale Road. Designed and completed in 1904 by the Boston architectural firm of Shepley, Rutan & Coolidge, its classical details with recessed Ionic columns at the entrance and massive Palladian windows in the reading rooms made for an elegant town library.

Everyone loves a parade! As town residents line Canton Avenue outside the First Parish Church, Unitarian, the Colors are held high during Memorial Day exercises paying tribute to Milton's honored dead.

The Milton Women's Club was built on Reedsdale Road. The club, still going strong after decades of service to the community, has as its motto: "Unity of Action and Breadth of Thought."

Jason Reed, for whom Reedsdale Road was named, was the town clerk of Milton and later served as town treasurer.

The pond in Milton Cemetery has a bucolic quality, with mature shade trees lining its banks. Today, ducks, swans, and a wide variety of wildlife take refuge in this arboretum cemetery.

The original section of the Milton Cemetery was laid out in 1672 and added to over the next two centuries through bequests of land and expansion by the town. Here, slate headstones of the eighteenth century rise from the ground while a mound tomb (left) offers above ground accommodations for townsmen of a century ago.

School Street was named for the North School, which was located on it in the nineteenth century. This c. 1880 photograph of the street was taken from Canton Avenue.

Ruggles Lane, which connects Brook Road and Centre Street, was a dirt road with a distinctly country-like setting in the late nineteenth century.

The old Crossman House was on Hillside Street. Two men pose outside the salt box cottage at the turn of the century.

The Joseph Vose House was built in 1761 on Vose's Lane. Major Vose later served during the Revolution, and was brevetted a Brigadier General by the end of the war.

The Draper House is at the corner of Canton Avenue and Reedsdale Road. An impressive Italianate house, it was originally set on a large lot that was later subdivided, with two houses being built on the Reedsdale Road side of the property.

The Leeds House was on Central Avenue, near the police station. The Leeds family, including the family horse, posed proudly in this *c.* 1870 photograph.

The Hinckley House was located at 264 Brook Road. Built by the Mather family in the mid-eighteenth century, it was the home of Thomas Hewes Hinckley, a noted artist of animal portraits and "farmscapes." His studio, where he painted the great majority of his canvases, is on the right.

Thomas Hewes Hinckley (1813–1888) was born in the house at 264 Brook Road, and he painted the majority of his paintings there. It was said that the "scenery of his native town has furnished him abundant material for his brush. He has followed no artist or school of art; but has endeavored to represent nature as he saw it."

Turner's Pond on Central Avenue was named for Alanson Turner, an ice merchant. Turner was associated with James F. Pope in the Pope and Turner Ice Company, established in 1883.

Joseph McKean Churchill (1821–1886) was a member of the Churchill family, for whom Churchill's Lane was named. An active town meeting member, it was said of him that during "a period of twenty five years he served as moderator in the conduct of thirty-two meetings in town affairs." A member of the Massachusetts House of Representatives and of the Governor's Council under Governor Banks, he was serving as an associate justice of the Boston Municipal Court at the time of his death.

Union Veterans and members of the Grand Army of the Republic (GAR) pose outside the Milton Town Hall in 1912. Proudly wearing their GAR badges of office, these veterans of the Civil War always participated in the local Memorial Day exercises.

Members of the Milton Red Cross pose on the steps of their headquarters on Adams Street in 1944. The Milton Red Cross was located in the former Russell House from 1942 to 1946. Though most members wore their distinctive cap for this photograph, who was the young fellow in front?

Five
Thacher's Plain

Thacher's Plain is a level stretch of land extending from Canton Avenue to the Blue Hill Parkway. Once owned by the Reverend Peter Thacher, minister of the Milton church from 1681 to 1727, the land remained undeveloped until the late nineteenth century, when houses were built along Thacher Street (which can be seen in the background).

Known as "Town Field," the open land bounded by Brook Road and Thacher Street became a playground for the new neighborhood. A group of young girls are shown here dancing in the park while their parents, brothers, and friends watch from the sidelines. Today, the park is known as Kelly Field.

Maypoles were set up at Town Field for the rite of spring dances. These were performed by young girls, one of which would be crowned "Queen of the May." Though banned on Merrymount in Quincy in the seventeenth century, by the early twentieth century maypoles had been revived as a sentimental custom of the age old ritual of spring.

Sack races at Town Field were a popular event for young boys a century ago. With their legs wrapped in large burlap bags, boys would jump towards the finish line while being cheered on by their friends.

The Kidder Branch of the Milton Public Library was built in 1928 on the Blue Hills Parkway. It was constructed on the site of an old house that had formerly been used as a community center. Nathaniel Thayer Kidder donated the land; he also donated the land at East Milton for the branch built in 1931.

Blue Hill Avenue, which ran from Roxbury to Milton and was originally known as the Brush Hill Turnpike, had tollhouses at specific points where one would pay a toll according to the weight of one's cart. This old tollhouse at Brush Hill (Mattapan) was photographed in 1909, over sixty years after the road was declared free to all.

Kerrigan's Corner, shown here in 1910, is the junction of Reedsdale and Brook Roads and Central Avenue. The streetcar is a thirteen-bench double truck of the Old Colony Street Railway. Headed towards Mattapan Square, these open streetcars must have been pleasant during the summer months, but the winter must have been an abomination!

The paper mill of Edmund Tileston and Mark Hollingsworth was built in the early nineteenth century. Paper was manufactured in Milton as early as 1728, when Hugh McLean and James Boies commenced the processing of linen rags into paper that was later used for wills, documents, and currency.

Thatcher Farm is a dairy located on Thacher Street opposite Central Avenue. Here, horse-drawn milk wagons leave the dairy for the morning delivery of milk and cream. Still supplying Milton and surrounding communities with dairy products, Thatcher Farm is a well-known business.

The Jeremiah Smith Boies House was on the Blue Hills Parkway (formerly Mattapan Street), opposite the Kidder Branch of the Milton Public Library. Boies inherited his family's paper mill and operated it until he moved to Boston. In the early twentieth century, the estate became the Leopold Morse Home for Jewish orphans. After its demolition, the monumental Ionic columns were reused on a pair of two-family houses on Eliot Street near Mattapan.

The Blue Hills Parkway was originally known as Mattapan Street. The center strip of green lawn was laid out from Mattapan to Canton Avenue in the 1930s. Trees were planted in a regular formation, creating an impressive alley as one drove in either direction.

Six

Cunningham Park

The Edward Cunningham Estate was a fairly self-sufficient farm of 150 acres in Milton. The farm's flocks of sheep not only added greatly to the charm of the fields, but could be shorn for their wool. Although Reverend Francis and Mary Forbes Cunningham had lived in great comfort, Mrs. Cunningham "left practically the whole of her considerable fortune to three trustees to be utilized for the benefit of the inhabitants of Milton. The trustees established and ever since have operated Cunningham Park with funds made available by her generous bequest." The park first opened in 1905.

The Cunningham House, formerly Dr. Amos Holbrook's house, was on Adams Street, overlooking Hutchinson Field. The dining room of the house had a domestic quality, and featured fine antiques mixed with comfortable arm chairs and ivy plants that wound their way up and over a pier mirror.

Cunningham Pool is provided for the residents of Milton by the income of the Cunningham Fund. During the summer, children can swim in this pool where "not everyone can be a champion, but all can enjoy participation in a splendid sport."

Ice skating and races have been enjoyed at Cunningham Park ever since the land was laid out. Here racers skate while being cheered on by the crowd.

A gymkhana, a meet featuring a sports race, was held at Cunningham Park during the town celebration of 1912. From left to right, the riders are: Philip Chase, Miss Josephine Griffith, Mrs. Walter D. Brooks, Miss Dorothea Hughes, Miss Hildegard Cobb, Miss Marian Weld, Miss Mildred Hastings, and Dr. Stanley Cobb. Walter D. Brooks is standing by the barrel at the left, with his horse beside him.

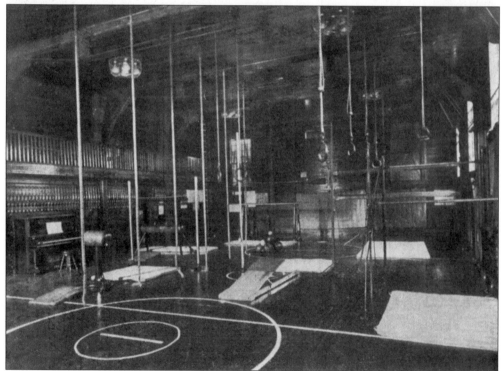

The gymnasium of Cunningham Park was a well-equipped facility open to all Milton residents. Open daily, the pool and park, provided almost a century ago through the generosity of Mary Forbes Cunningham, still benefit the people of Milton.

Seven

Canton Avenue

During the late nineteenth century, Canton Avenue was a main thoroughfare to the towns south of Milton. From early in the century, the houses built on the road were of grand dimensions. Markets such as the Blue Hill Market near the corner of Robbins Street serviced these residents.

Many houses get their name from the family which was the most prominent or which resided in the house for the longest period. This house, the home of Alpheus Babcock, was later occupied by the Armstrong and Crouse families but is still known locally as the Babcock House.

The Tucker family has been a part of Milton history since Robert Tucker settled on Brush Hill in 1662. Reverend Teele, author of *The History of Milton 1640–1887*, relates there that a continuous line of Ephraim Tucker's descendants served as deacons of the church from 1699 to 1887. Others served in the army and in representative assemblies of the nation. Atherton Tucker, shown here, was a resident of the Canton Avenue area and a distinguished leader in the field of investments in the latter part of the nineteenth century.

Emanuel Sutermeister developed a thriving commercial vegetable garden and plant nursery on the site of what came to be known as the Davenport-Sutermeister House. His daughter Margaret was an early photographer who showed great skill and sensitivity in her work. The Milton Historical Society recently published a collection of her photography. Upon the death of Emanuel, Margaret ended her photographic avocation and assumed the management of the family business.

A typical middle class family—the Sutermeisters—is shown here in the nineteenth century, sitting in the parlor and enjoying each others company. Notice the readily available reading matter, which would be at hand for family discussions.

Emanuel Sutermeister inspects the the burgeoning plants that thrive in his greenhouse on Canton Avenue.

The Sutermeister garden business required much physical labor. Pictured here is a group of the farmhands who did the laborious work, first under the supervision of Emanuel, and later under the supervision of his daughter Margaret.

Work on a farm was hard and never seemed to end, but at least this worker could proffer an engaging smile.

The large homes built in the Canton Avenue area housed families of some material means who were able to hire the help necessary to maintain their homes and grounds. This picture shows the maid taking advantage of sunny weather to do the family washing.

This house was located at 23 Robbins Street. Records indicate that it was built by Manassah Tucker about 1707, and that the photograph was taken in 1899.

This photograph of the house at the corner of Canton Avenue and Atherton Street sparks an interest because of its subtle details. From the use of the shutters we know it was a sunny day, yet the people depicted were fully clothed, in keeping with the style of that time. The connecting passage to the barn provided a sheltered work site near the entrance of the granite block cellar.

A horse-drawn pung heads south on Canton Avenue. The image evokes the thought that "the horse knows the way . . ."

The Meadowbrook cart was a distinctive vehicle for a lady seeking a pleasant afternoon's diversion. The cart's large wheels permitted passage over fairly rough terrain without discomfort to the rider, and it was usually drawn by the gentlest of horses.

The Russell House was built on what was the original site of Colonel Miller's residence. Miller's home was completely destroyed by fire in 1770, and Miller, because he had sided with the Loyalists, lost his land. Later, Henry Sturgis Russell constructed the impressive mansion shown here. Russell was a colonel in the Civil War and was brevetted a Brigadier General. He served both as the police and fire commissioner of Boston and held several public offices in Milton.

This room in Dr. John Sprague's home at 1350 Canton Avenue was a typical sedate parlor at the beginning of the nineteenth century. In the early twentieth century, the building was the home of Hannah Palfrey and James B. Ayer, who moved the Suffolk Resolves House to its present site.

This grand and imposing house was designed by William Ralph Emerson of Milton and is known as the William-Ellery-Channing-Eustis House. Built at 1426 Canton Avenue, it is still occupied by the Eustis family.

This house, located near Dollar Lane on Canton Avenue, sheltered the Wainwright family through the Victorian era. Note the hand-held scythe used by the groundskeeper.

This graciously proportioned house at 1733 Canton Avenue was home to Roger Walcott, who served as governor of Massachusetts during the Spanish-American War.

Roger Walcott (1847–1901) was a distinguished member of the Massachusetts bar who spent much of his professional career as a trustee of estates. He was a leader in many civic and charitable causes in Milton. Walcott served as lieutenant-governor of the Commonwealth from 1892 to 1895, and governor from 1896 to 1898.

Eight
Highland Street

Edward Cunningham, after making a fortune in the China trade, retired to Milton and built this house just after the Civil War. In 1889 he died as a result of being shot by a wood poacher on his 150-acre estate. His home later became the Milton Hospital and Convalescent Home. It was located on the hill above what eventually became the skating rink in Cunningham Park. The park was created by the trustees of a fund established by his aunt, Mary Forbes Cunningham. The Convalescent Home continued in operation until the initial section of the present Milton Hospital was built.

This view of the Cunningham House shows it as it was with convalescents and workers in the late nineteenth century.

The patients at the Convalescent Home were frequently visited by townspeople, including these high school girls, who went a' caroling at Christmas time.

This view of the Convalescent Home shows it in its majestic setting.

The original part of what is now Milton Medical Center was dedicated in September 1950. It opened a new era of medical care in Milton and led to the demise of the former Convalescent Home.

The original buildings of Bent Cracker were simple structures where water crackers were baked daily in wall ovens.

Bent's cracker factory was established in 1801 by Josiah Bent, who was reputed to have made the first water crackers in America. The company has continued with changes in ownership and location, as well as changes in the assortment of bakery goods offered for sale. Pictured here is Arthur Pierotti, owner and baker, "feeding the oven" in a photograph dating from the 1940s.

Built in 1802 by Bezer Thayer, a farmer who also did some cobbling, this house is now occupied by Robert Oldfield, the owner of Thayer Nursery. Mr. Oldfield served the town as a member of the school committee, and has been a town meeting member for some years. The photograph dates from the turn of the century.

The General Vose House on Highland Street was set on a large estate.

Samuel Adams came to Milton from Bath, Maine, in 1806. From his home (shown above) he became a tin maker and had a small shop. He served in the "Boston Rangers" during the War of 1812 and married into the Bent bakery family. In 1834, when the Unitarian Church was formed, Samuel Adams was elected deacon and continued to hold this office for forty five years, until his death.

The formal gardens of the Whitney Estate on Highland Street included sunken gardens, waterfalls, and glorious flower beds that bloomed three seasons of the year.

Nine
Brush Hill Road

Robert Tucker came here from Milton-Near-Gravesend, England, and built this house in 1670 on the west side of what is now Brush Hill Road. It was later moved to the east side of the road, and dormers were added in the nineteenth century. At that time it was named "Overbrook." During its history it has also been known as the Clark House and the Whitney Carr House.

Shortly before the town's first settlers arrived, a forest fire destroyed all the trees on the west side of town. The hill was quickly covered with brush: hence the name of the area. The Robbins House on Brush Hill Road at the corner of Smith Street was built by James Murray, a Loyalist, long before the Revolutionary War. In 1805 the house was acquired by Edward Hutchinson Robbins, the founder of Milton Academy.

One of the early homes on Brush Hill was the Amor Hollingsworth House. Tradition teaches that the site for this building was chosen because of the well. It was the home of a local papermaker.

This photograph of Brush Hill was taken from Canton Avenue at the turn of the century.

This is a pastoral view of the house that stood next to the Ferry House. It was taken by the photographer (whose shadow looms before us) shortly before the tree was felled and the barn torn down.

The Amor Hollingsworth House was located on Brush Hill Road. A substantial Italianate mansion set on spacious grounds, the estate was subdivided in this century with Amor Street bisecting the grounds.

The beautiful house at 311 Brush Hill Road was set on extensive grounds. The sweeping carriage drive leads to a house on the left.

"Meadowbrook Cottage" was built by Mary Goddard White, and it was later the home of W. Rodman Peabody. This photograph of the house was taken from Bradlee Road. Like the other houses in the area, it fronted on Brush Hill Road.

The governess and her charges were photographed in a Meadowbrook cart on Bradlee Road.

George Shaw, who later established the distinguished Boston architectural firm of Perry, Shaw and Hepburn, was the architect who designed this house, while the grounds including the drive were laid out by Frederick Law Olmstead. It was known as the Charles Goddard White House.

Mrs. Charles Goddard White, Frank White (her son), and faithful Rowe are shown here on the piazza of the White House on a summer afternoon.

Ten

Milton Schools

The Old West School was on Blue Hill Avenue near Atherton Street. Built in 1812, it was known as the "Old Brick." It was demolished in 1870.

The counterpart of the West School was the East School. Built in 1862 on land near the corner of Squantum and Adams Streets, it later became part of the Saint Agatha Parish complex.

This unusual photograph shows the students of the East School at the time of the Civil War posing on the porch and roof of the school.

This very old school building once stood on Adams Street. It now serves as the Children's Church at the First Parish Church, Unitarian, on the corner of Canton Avenue and Thacher Street.

BELCHER SCHOOL
EAST MILTON, MASS.
0283

The Belcher School was a wood-shingled building built in 1894 on a granite foundation at the site of the East School in East Milton. The school was named after Royal Governor Jonathan Belcher and his family, who settled here in the mid-seventeenth century.

Vose School, Milton, Mass.   529

The Milton High School was built in 1910 at the corner of Brook Road and Central Avenue. Originally known as the Vose School, it has been considerably enlarged over the years and today dwarfs this original building.

The Glover School is at the corner of Canton Avenue and Brook Road.

The Vose School was built in 1885 and was originally behind the old town hall on Canton Avenue. A massive Romanesque Revival building that served as Milton High School until 1910, it had three stories and large classrooms for the swelling population of Milton schoolchildren. A horse-drawn buggy is drawn up in front of the entrance.

This 1950s photograph of a "Teen Night" in Milton features dancing "bobby sockers" enjoying a Friday night social at the high school.

The Milton High School Class of 1956 had its graduation exercises in the new gym. Shown here as if they were new graduates posing on bleachers before their family and friends, these class members celebrate their 40th anniversary in 1996!

Prior to the completion of the new gym at the Milton High School, graduation exercises were held outdoors, weather permitting! A line of graduates—with their mortarboards on—walk in formation from the school to their seats.

The old Milton Academy building stood on Canton Avenue at the rear of the First Parish Church, Unitarian. Chartered in 1798, the first building was completed in 1806. The school accommodated twenty-three boys from Milton and the surrounding towns.

Christopher Greene served as preceptor, or headmaster, of Milton Academy.

The entrance to Milton Academy from Randolph Avenue has a small shingle-style house just inside the gates.

An all-girls school, Ware Hall was built on Centre Street at the corner of Randolph Avenue. Named for Harriet Ware, a benefactress of Milton Academy and a trustee from 1879 to 1912, its classical details make it an impressive building.

The campus of Milton Academy, seen from the driveway leading off Randolph Avenue, seems to welcome the serious student. Harrison Otis Apthorp "laid the foundations upon which a great school was built." His widow built Apthorp Chapel, and its crenelated tower can be seen here on the left.

Howard Abel conducts the Milton Academy girl's school chorus during graduation exercises in 1951.

Fontbonne Academy is located on Centre Street in a modern school building.

Milton Little League players stand at attention in 1952 as the National Anthem is sung prior to the game. Since 1951, the activity of the Milton Little League has provided several generations of Milton children with an opportunity to play organized baseball.

Eleven

Milton Worships

The First Parish Church, Unitarian, was built in 1787 on Canton Avenue. The fourth meetinghouse to be built, it is now at a right angle to its original position. Originally built as a Congregational meetinghouse, it became Unitarian by vote of the church membership. Prior to the adoption of the Eleventh Amendment to the Massachusetts Constitution, town meetings were held here.

The town-wide celebration in 1912 of the 250th anniversary of Milton brought residents to the First Parish Church, Unitarian, for an afternoon of festivities including a concert, speeches, and an historical pageant.

At the 250th Anniversary Celebration of Milton, members of the First Parish Church, Unitarian, had a lawn party, complete with Japanese lanterns strung for illumination. Here, members of the church pose on the side of the property.

The First Congregational Church in Milton was gathered after the First Parish adopted Unitarianism. Built on the opposite end of the Milton Town Hall, it is an impressive church.

The East Congregational Church was built on Adams Street in East Milton, which was known as "Railway Village" in the mid-nineteenth century. The church served the needs of those who worked in the granite industry, but has now been remodeled into condominiums.

The East Congregational Church, seen from across Adams Street, had a small but active congregation of eighteen men and women when it was established in 1843. The congregation built this meetinghouse in 1846. After 1951 the building was used as the Elks Lodge. It has recently been adapted as condominiums.

The new East Milton Congregational Church was built opposite the original church and dedicated on September 23, 1951. The new church, located at the corner of Adams and Church Streets, has gracious and classical dimensions with a soaring spire that adds greatly to the area of East Milton.

Saint Michael's Episcopal Church was built in 1896 on Randolph Avenue, one year after the organization of the parish. Designed by local architect Ralph Lincoln Emerson, there are stones in the arch from Boston, England, and from the ancient church in Milton Abbas, Dorset, England.

As the number of Episcopal communicants grew in Milton, the need for a new church became apparent, and in 1897 a mission church was established at East Milton. It later became the Church of Our Savior. The joyous occasion of the laying of the cornerstone occurred in 1914.

The Church of Our Savior on Adams Street in East Milton does not look much different today than it did eighty years ago.

The choir of the Church of Our Savior included Reverend Reese, who at the time served as the pastor of Saint Michael's and the Church of Our Savior. He later became a bishop of Ohio.

This small wood-framed building was the first meetinghouse of the Baptist congregation in East Milton. It was once part of the East School and was moved to Bryant Avenue in 1886.

As the East Milton Baptist Church congregation grew, the need for a larger church led to the erection of this shingle-style building in 1893.

The Parkway Methodist Church was established on the Boston side of Mattapan in 1844. This imposing fieldstone church was erected in 1926 on the Blue Hills Parkway.

The original Saint Elizabeth's Church was a reconstructed servicemen's chapel brought from Camp Myles Standish in Taunton, Massachusetts. Purchased from the federal government for $1 and erected across the street from the present church, it was dedicated in 1947 as a living memorial of Milton's honored dead.

Saint Agatha's was initially a mission of Saint Gregory's parish in the Dorchester Lower Mills. In 1922, it was established as a separate parish, with the Reverend Eugene A. Carney serving as pastor. A fine example of a Gothic church built on locally-quarried granite, it is an impressive addition to East Milton.

The Saint Mary of the Hills parish was formed in 1931 and the church was erected on Saint Mary's Road in 1934. The Catholic population of Milton continued to expand, and by the 1950s there were three parishes in Milton: Saint Agatha's, Saint Elizabeth's, and Saint Mary of the Hills.

Temple B'Nai Jacob is located at 100 Blue Hills Parkway. It was formed in 1960 so that believers could bring to their worship the rituals of Hebraic Orthodoxy.

Temple Shalom was erected in 1943 on Blue Hill Avenue to serve those faithful to the Hebraic tradition in the Conservative manner.

Twelve
Public Safety

As Milton grew from a remote farming community into a country town with many well-to-do Bostonians moving here, law enforcement grew to include a full-fledged uniformed police force. The first police station, built in 1884 at the town landing, can be seen in the background. This photograph shows the entire police force as it was manned in 1905. The old station house is now the home of the Milton Yacht Club.

MILTON SOCIETY
—FOR—
APPREHENDING HORSE THIEVES.

At the annual meeting of the Society in Milton for Apprehending Horse Thieves, and the Recovery of Stolen Horses, held at the Town House, Jan.   , 186   , the following persons were elected Officers for the year ensuing:

SAMUEL COOK, President.   **GEORGE K. GANNETT, Vice President.**

THOMAS T. WADSWORTH, Treasurer.

STANDING COMMITTEE.

SAMUEL ADAMS,	LEWIS DAVENPORT,	LEONARD MORSE,	DANA TUCKER,
LEMUEL W. BABCOCK,	HENRY G. DURELL,	JOHN W. PORTER,	NATHAN TUCKER,
JOSIAH BABCOCK,	NATHAN HOLBROOK,	GEORGE RAYMOND,	ELIJAH TUCKER,
CHARLES BRECK,	CHARLES HUNT,	JAMES M. ROBBINS,	TIMOTHY TUCKER,
EBENEZER CURTIS,	AMOR HOLLINGSWORTH,	E. H. R. RUGGLES,	THOMAS T. WADSWORTH.
LEWIS COPELAND,	THOMAS HOLLIS,	ROBERT M. TODD,	

RIDERS.

SAMUEL BABCOCK,	WILLIAM B. CLEMENTS,	GEORGE K. GANNETT,	GEORGE W. HALL,	JOHN SIAS,
CORNELIUS BABCOCK,	NATHAN CROSSMAN, Jr.,	SAMUEL GANNETT,	DAVID G. HICKS,	TIMOTHY TUCKER,
JOSIAH S. BEALE,	SAMUEL COOK,	CHARLES K. HUNT,	JOHN MYERS,	DANA TUCKER,
JOHN D. BRADLEE,	MOSES CHAPMAN,	JOHN A. HAVEN,	JOHN W. PORTER,	JOHN W. THACHER,
A. D. CAPEN,	N. T. DAVENPORT,	NATHAN HOLBROOK,	LABAN PRATT,	JOSIAH F. TWOMBLY,
JOHN J. CLAPP,	LEWIS DAVENPORT,		JOHN P. REED,	JOSHUA W. VOSE,
CHARLES L. COPELAND,	BENJAMIN F. DUDLEY,		HENRY V. SHEPARD,	JOSIAH WEBB.

NAMES OF MEMBERS.

MILTON.

Samuel Adams,
Joseph Angier,
Widow Nathaniel Bent,
Samuel Babcock,
Cornelius Babcock,
John D. Bradlee,
James Breck,
Charles Breck,
Thomas S. Briggs,
Jonathan Beale,
Henry Beal,
John H. Burt,
Lemuel W. Babcock,
Widow Cephas Belcher,
Edward Baldwin,

Lewis J. Clap,
Edwin Clapp,
A. E. Capen,
Nathan Crossman, Jr.,
Charles L. Copeland,
Lewis Copeland,
John Collamore, Jr.,
William H. Davis,
Widow Wm. Davenport,
Lewis Davenport,
Nathaniel T. Davenport,
Henry G. Durell,
William Davis,
James H. Dudley,
B. F. Dudley,
Robert M. Edwards,
Samuel Everett,

Widow Isaac Gulliver,
David G. Hicks,
Amor Hollingsworth,
Andrew Hobson,
Thomas Hollis,
Christopher C. Holmes,
Widow Samuel Holmes,
Charles K. Hunt,
Widow Thomas Hunt, Jr.,
George W. Hall,
Adolphus Kinsman,
Charles Larkin,
Samuel Littlefield,
Nathan C. Martin,
Widow Joseph Morton,
Leonard Morse,
John Myers,

Benjamin S. Rotch,
E. Samuel,
Henry V. Shepard,
Lemuel Sumner,
Widow James Semple,
Eliphalet Sias,
John Sias,
George Skinner,
Widow Dean M. Swift,
Widow Charles Sloan,
John W. Thacher,
Dana Tucker,
Elijah Tucker,
Nathan Tucker,
Jesse Tucker,
Timothy Tucker,
Robert V. Tucker,

Joshua W. Vose,
Widow Moses Whitney,
Jonathan Ware,
Josiah Wadsworth,
Thomas T. Wadsworth,
Widow Barney S. Wilde,
Seth D. Whitney,
Josiah Webb,
John Williams.

DORCHESTER.

E. J. Baker,
James Brown,
Widow Simon Brown,
Widow Darius Brewer,
A. D. Capen,

Micah Humphrey,
Charles Hunt,
John A. Haven,
Edward T. Howe,
John Kendrick,
Thomas Liversidge,
Henry Liversidge,
Joseph Marshall, 2d,
Widow John Preston,
Henry L. Pierce,
Widow W. Pierce,
Lewis F. Pierce,
Thomas Pierce,
John W. Porter,
Laban Pratt,
E. H. R. Ruggles,
Robert Rhodes,

Widow R. P. Tolman,
Minot Thayer,
William E. Weeman,
Otis Wright.

CANTON.

George O. Downes,
Widow Jesse Davenport,
John Davenport,
Thomas French,
Widow John Gerald,
James T. Sumner,
Francis Sturtevant,
William Tucker.

QUINCY.

Before the growth of a police department, volunteers would band together to protect their most valuable possession—horses! Horses provided both transportation and work power; the loss of a horse could be equated with the loss of livelihood. This was a broadside of the "Milton Society for Apprehending Horse Thieves" that was prominently displayed around town, in order to, hopefully, discourage horse thieves.

The horse-drawn steam pumper of the Milton Fire Department is shown here parked outside the steam fire engine house in 1881. A major advance in fighting fires, steam pumpers no longer required volunteers to man the hand-powered pump. Horse power was used instead, so that firefighters were free to do other things. Edward Pierce Hamilton, author of *A History of Milton*, relates that in 1896 Milton's fire department was considered the finest in Massachusetts, excepting Boston.

This turn-of-the-century photograph shows the members of the Milton Fire Department in front of the old fire house behind the First Congregational Church. One wonders if facial hair was necessary to be a good firefighter!

Steamer #19 is shown here in all its glory in front of the Mattapan station.

Firefighters pose with the horse-drawn steam pumper and hose wagon in front of the Central Station behind town tall. The last horse of the Milton Fire Department was replaced by motor vehicle apparatus in 1919, so the horses in this c. 1920 photograph had to be borrowed from Thatcher Farm to "recreate" the pre-World War I equipment.

Hose Company No. 2 was based in East Milton. Members of the firehouse pose in front of the building in a horse-drawn hose wagon.

Hose Company No. 2 is shown here in a more formal pose, with the firemen in their dress uniforms. Even the horses seem to be standing at attention for the photographer!

The sparkling new gas engine-powered fire engine heralded modern times for the Milton Fire Department. Note the solid rubber tires and the length of the hood in relation to the body of the fire truck.

Horses for the mounted police patrols around the wooded hills of Milton were stabled adjacent to this stone building. Later, the horses were replaced by motor vehicles, and the entire police effort of the Metropolitan District Commission became part of the state police. This building is now a station for the Massachusetts State Police.

Thirteen
Blue Hills

Houghton's Pond is located at the south of Great Blue Hill in the Blue Hills Reservation. The old Indian name for the pond was Hoosic Whisick, which is perpetuated in the name of a club on Central Avenue.

Ralph Houghton's house at Houghton's Pond was a typical Milton farmhouse in 1888.

This stone bridge, gracefully arching over the Neponset River, is known as Paul's Bridge. It is named after the Paul family, who owned land on the Dedham side of the Neponset River, and was originally made of wood. The stone bridge was built in 1840, and when it was later rebuilt, many of the original stones were reused. It looks almost exactly the same today as it does in this 1921 photograph.

Photographed at the turn of the century, a mother and daughter refresh themselves at the drinking water fountain before their climb in the Blue Hills.

A group of friends enjoy watermelon slices after having reached the summit of Great Blue Hill. In the background is a structure erected by A. Lawrence Rotch for meteorological research. This site became the location of the oldest continuously-used weather station in the nation. At a later time, the name served as the basis for the "call letters" of WGBH.

Dr. A. Lawrence Rotch (1861–1912), on the right, and an assistant are shown here preparing an experiment on temperature and humidity in the upper air using a Hargrave Box Kite.

Dr. Rotch (center) readies an instrument-bearing ballon which will radio back weather conditions from a high altitude. The first airborne recording thermometer was set up by Rotch in 1894.

The opening of the Blue Hills Ski Slope in the late 1930s brought skiers from far and wide. Looking down the fabricated snow-covered ski jump, we see spectators intently watching a skier who has glissaded and is now airborne.

Wendell Phillips, a distinguished lecturer and a leading abolitionist prior to the Civil War, was the brother-in-law of Robert Bennet Forbes. He is buried in the Milton Cemetery on Centre Street.

The family of Walter Scott Davis resided on Canton Avenue. This photograph of him in full dress was taken shortly before his promotion to the rank of colonel during the Civil War.

124

Fourteen
Fellow Townsmen

Edmund J. Baker (1805–1890) was the grandson of Daniel Vose and Dr. James Baker, the founder of the Baker Chocolate Company. After an academic education, Edmund chose to be a surveyor and it was his 1831 survey map of Dorchester and Milton that was often used for land disputes in the nineteenth century. He was one of the founders of the Dorchester Historic and Antiquarian Society, and served as its president from 1872 until his death in1890. He was a justice of the peace and the trustee of many estates, as well as president of the Dorchester Mutual Fire Insurance Company.

Mrs. Crossman, photographed at a great age, "takes the air" in her doorway.

Nathaniel Foster Safford was a prominent attorney who was active in local affairs. A long-time Norfolk County Commissioner, he was host to Congressman Abraham Lincoln when he visited Dorchester Lower Mills in 1848 to campaign for Zachary Taylor. His estate, known as "Brookmount," was on Westside Road.

Henry Parsons Kidder was a prosperous merchant whose estate was on Adams Street on Milton Hill. In 1886, he established the first trust for the benefit of the Milton Public Library. His son, Nathaniel Thayer Kidder, was chairman of the trustees for many years and was the library's most generous benefactor.

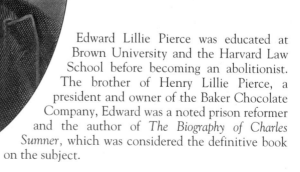

Edward Lillie Pierce was educated at Brown University and the Harvard Law School before becoming an abolitionist. The brother of Henry Lillie Pierce, a president and owner of the Baker Chocolate Company, Edward was a noted prison reformer and the author of *The Biography of Charles Sumner*, which was considered the definitive book on the subject.

Dr. Christopher Columbus Holmes was one of Milton's principal physicians in the late nineteenth century. A noted and accomplished musician, he also served as captain in the First Corps of Cadets in Boston.

Eleanor Pope Martin was photographed with her dog "Leo" in 1876. As an adult, she showed a strong interest in early Milton history and wrote several papers on the subject which are in the collection of the Milton Historical Society. She also established the Martin Fund and the Audubon Sanctuary on Maple Street, which was discontinued after her death in 1957.